the Queen Elizabeth
May 2015

A Shed for Wood

DANIEL THOMAS MORAN

salmonpoetry

Published in 2014 by
Salmon Poetry
Cliffs of Moher, County Clare, Ireland
Website: www.salmonpoetry.com
Email: info@salmonpoetry.com

Paperback ISBN 978-1-908836-61-8

Cover Photography: Daniel T. Moran
Typesetting & Cover Design: Siobhán Hutson

"The youth gets together his materials to build a bridge to the moon, or, perchance, a palace or temple on the earth, and, at length the middle-aged man concludes to build a wood-shed with them."

HENRY DAVID THOREAU

*This book is dedicated to the memory of
Samuel Menashe, Allen Planz and Siv Cedering,
admired poets and dear friends.*

*And, as always,
with love to Karen.*

Acknowledgements

Poems in this collection have been previously published in *Poetry Salzburg Review, Ars Poetica, Asinine Poetry, Black Cat Poems, Black/In The Red Anthology, Confrontation, East River Review, Hawaii Pacific Review, Humanist Living, Humanist Network News, Impressions, In Our Words/ A Generation Defining Itself — The 60's, Istanbul Literature Review, Mobius, Nomad's Choir, Opium, Palehouse, Poetry pRo at The University of Bucharest, Translation Café at The University of Bucharest, Rebel Road Anthology, Street Magazine, Whorl, POETRY tREnD Anthology/ Ludwig Maximilions University of Munich, Medical Humanities Journal, Hektoen International, Literary Matters* (Association of Literary Scholars, Critics and Writers), *Exit 13* and *Sfera Eonica* (Romania).

Contents

FOREWORD

Daniel Moran's poetic arms reach effortlessly from the quotidian to the empyrean, bringing us, on the one hand, a down-to-earth landscape of sun and rain, dust and mud, herons and sandpipers, fireflies and mayflies – and, on the other hand, the wide world of Ireland and India and Pompeii, a world of gods and paradise, life and loving, fear and dying. Unlike some contemporary poetry, Moran's poems are always about something, and he doesn't adulterate his observations with stylish syntactical stunts or pseudo-profundity.

No subject is more suited to poetry than love, and Moran celebrates it in the best ways possible; by writing some powerfully honest words to his wife Karen, then yielding to an eloquent silence:

> *I love you* is not enough.
> Some things defy the naming.
> Let me rest my head
> on your shoulder, and
> rest yours on mine.
> Take my glance, it
> contains much more.
> I have no words
> more true, more tender
> than what is found
> in that vast silence.

Love and death, so antithetical in life, are rivals for the attention of poets, and Moran pays his respects to both:

> Some of my friends
> seem to be wearing out,
> their pink becoming gray,
> their tightness loosened.
> Some will be told today.

And occasionally in his poems the dance of death becomes literal, tangible, and chillingly oppressive:

> Even as we live it is
> the dead we romance,
> leading them onto
> the ballroom floor...
> We guide them in
> slow and careful circles.
> Over the lacquered wood.
> Our cheeks pressed to theirs.
> There is something
> about that cold.
> And the eyes.
> Like unlit rooms.

Thoughts of death sometimes bring on thoughts about religion, but Moran doesn't take that subject too seriously.

> His eye is
> upon
> the sparrow
> But the sparrow
> has
> no clue.
> The sparrow,
> unlike
> The Almighty,
> Has
> more important
> things
> to do.

And in "It's like OMG," he writes:

> My children
> use their thumbs
> to converse with
> invisible people.
> They speak
> a language with
> no words...
> and God exists
> as a single letter.

Pondering the fundamentalists' notion of "Intelligent Design," he concludes:

> I have faith
> that it would
> be wholly
> mistakable
> to endorse any
> god who'd make
> a bone that
> was breakable.

As is clear from these lines, Moran not only has important things to say, but he has fun saying them. His poem to the Mayfly reflects on life's tragic brevity, but, flexing his rhyming skills, he looks on the bright side:

> Among the simple Mayfly facts is,
> He never once has to file his taxes.

And even with that ancient survivor, the horseshoe crab, Moran sees a reason to be upbeat:

> Tumbling in love, in the surf,
> You might think that they'll botch it.
> But when the dinosaurs died out,
> They were right there to watch it.

Clearly, Moran has his poet's eye not only on sparrows but on everything that moves around him, or that simply moves him – and then, thanks to his skill and talent, moves us. This book takes a clear, serious, and amusing look at it all, and offers us good reasons for hope.

PHILIP APPLEMAN

At Davisville, New Hampshire

Here is the place I have found,
of fertile earth between tumbled stone.

Where old men lean thick arms
upon the tails of pick-ups,
on autumn mornings and others,
and settle the matters of a day.

Where water spills from mountains,
over and down between hills,
and breaths, on winter nights
are seized by the gelid air.

Where the firmament
and all of its tiny lights,
lie upon the reach of treetops.

Where we can be with our aloneness,
at rest with its bottomless still,
and inhabit the life which inhabits us.

Christmas Eve at The Waldorf=Astoria

New York City, 2006

Jesus brought our bags
up to Room 805
at a little after 3.

He stayed
only long enough
to show us
the mini-bar, and
how to manage
the thermostat.

He let us know
that room service
would bring whatever
we desired.
Around the clock.

He was shorter
than I might have
imagined from those
paintings of Caravaggio,
and all of the
crucifixes of my childhood.

Hair sable, and newly cut,
He wore a gray uniform,
like the others in His place,
alive to serve mankind.

The outer edge
of His heels were
burnished by the miles
of pavement and carpet.

I wanted to ask Him
about The War,
and the crying babies
in East Harlem.
The dripping glaciers,
and where to find
a thing like Justice
in a world turning itself
inside out.

I wanted to know
if He could ever recall
sixty-three degrees
in New York City, at
the tail end of December.

But, I did not wish
to add to
His burden.

The Lobby
was teeming with
Italians and Minnesotans
and French and
Asians of many kinds.
All staring up
each time the chimes
rolled out from that
fabled golden clock.

There was only time,
to press a folded five
into His palm,
to thank Him
for bearing the weight
for us who are travelers.

And He smiled
in a way which
reassured me that

Somehow,
Everything
would be
all right.

Intelligent Design

for Christopher Hitchens

I cannot give
much credence
to divine
intervention,

Even at the
risk of my
defying
a redemption.

But I have faith
that it would
be wholly
mistakable,

To endorse any
god who'd make
a bone that
was breakable.

Opening the Box of Sax Bledshine

for Graham Everett

Around 1 a.m.,

Karen said, even though she was there, that
she thought she could almost remember The 60's.
Graham said he could even remember
the exact moment The 60's ended.

I thought I could remember something as well.
For me, The 60's were over before they began.
I spent my youth making believe that was not true.

Last night, my sleep was cheated by the full moon.
I lay awake thinking of Kerouac and Dan Murray.
Karen on a '52 Panhead Hardtail, looking for Janis Joplin.

Many of my own years have now expired.
It is still hard for me to be entirely where I am.

Nonetheless, the three of us are here in lamplight.
We have agreed that it is a January night,
slowly becoming a January morning.
The woods are fast asleep in the
fluorescent blush of a burnished moon.

We are all lucky to be alive after
all of the living we have done.

The Horseshoe Crabs Mating along Delaware Bay

That old horseshoe crab,
among the oddest of creatures.
Defies those decidedly,
fond of fine features.

They're neither crab nor horse,
you cannot eat or shoe them.
And when seen on their back,
there ain't too much to them.

Tumbling in love in the surf,
you might think that they'll botch it.
But when the dinosaurs died out,
they were right there to watch it.

The Book of Prophecy

I have been given
a datebook I cannot use.
It's a handsome thing.
Unpretentious, portable
and prepared for utility.
I even like its deep red cover,
which encases a future
I hope to see.

There is a blue ribbon
I could use to separate,
the what has been, from
the what's yet to be.

If I cannot find
someone in need of it, it
will have to remain barren.
Forever trapped by
a measure of time
it cannot escape.

The fortunate truth is that
I have a nice black one.
Soft and supple, perfect
for a back pocket or a
small corner of my nightstand,
and already populated by
my anticipations.

In a year's time, it will be
worthless and worn, papers
curled and consumed by
The totality of one man's
blue scribblings, and his hope
of making the future unforgettable.

The River Might Be a Woman

Here, in the first days
along our share of
the Warner River,
I have begun to believe,
that the river is, perhaps,
a beautiful woman.

Nevertheless, it seems
to be a metaphor
going nowhere. But,

The sight of her,
lying along this gentle slope.
The feeling of her,
reclined in the dark beside me.

It has captivated me
in ways which are
not so obvious, and which
do not lend themselves
to my feeble pryings.

I am content with that.
And I want to be
free to marvel.

But I confess,
I also want to touch it.
As a child wants
to touch a candle flame,
or a draping of
magenta velvet.

And then, as a man,
I want to be inside.

To The Generals

for Gregory Riordan Moran

You must take.
It is your nature.

You must
take down
take away
take leave.

You must
empty and spend,
even waste.

We have come to see
You will not be denied.
But please is all I can say.

Do Not Take My Son.

Not his legs or arms,
Not an eye or thumb,
Not his heart or his mind.

He is not yours to spend.

Should you insist,
you should know,

I could not face
one day more, knowing
that I had let you do it.

Some of My Friends

Some of my friends
are becoming concerned.

About lumps where there
were none before.
Some thing which
does not look right.
Their comforts
undermined by
pains sharp or dull.
The need to draw breath
into deeper places.

Some are feeling vulnerable.

Their eyes are clouding,
words appearing to dissolve.
Sounds soft and muffled.
Some of my friends
need procedures and
further testing.
They will have to
travel to someplace
far and unfamiliar
and wait.

They will try to recall
when sleep came easy.

Now they might have
to be kept overnight,
have blood let by
girls named Betty.
Lie beneath beams
which will turn their
skin to rice paper.
All of their functions
will be distilled
to graphs and digits.

Some of my friends
seem to be wearing out.
Their pink becoming gray.
Their tightness loosened.
Some will be told, today.

Scriptures

Of all to be said
Of gods and men,
Drawing truth from
The sharpened quill.

Are the many ways
They write of love,
And the ease
With which they kill.

The Master Makes a Line

My youth made
dancers move.
The curtain up,
beauty and poise
spinning within
the purple shades
of candles.

With my oils
I made them delicate
and strong, possessed of
inexhaustible youth.

Then there were
the ladies,
hundreds of them,
each one anxious
to recline before me.

Now I sit,
captured in this room,
betrayed by clocks.
Legs all but useless,
hands twisted as knots.

I must ask
my young girl
to strap a stick
to my arm, and
coax open the
bottle of ink.

I will show her
how it can be,
that a man can still
possess his gift.

That even
a single line,
can become
a miracle.

Thinking about the Death of John Updike

Out there in the world,
some brittle oak leaves
have survived the worst of it.
They cling, like the rest of us,
beset and shivering on
threads in March's wind.

The sun barely changes,
traipsing as it does, from
south to north and
then to south again.
And the blueness of the sky?
Well, what has not already
been well said about that?

I am listening
to the punk squelching
of Patti Smith, wriggling
in her tender agonies,
on a filthy stage on
The Bowery thirty-four
long years ago.

The heat has kicked on, and
a manufactured comfort
swirls up from the registers.
It is not the wind moving
outside that I think I hear.

In the slick pages of
the newest *New Yorker*,
something has pushed
up through the hard soil.
And I find myself living
the dying of John Updike.

The last of his poems have
lain down before me,
heads reclined into the
posed configuration of
a treacherous peace,
their toes pointed upward
toward ambiguous perpetuity.

I would have to say that
he was not so much unlike
any of us, we who have been
fated to finally become
the likeness of one another.

We believe what we
cannot understand and,
we know that we will go,
just as we came:
alone, wondering, and
empty handed.

The Blue Heron

Within the depiction
which is this river,

The Blue Heron is composed.

In the moving world,
like the rock which
is his perch,

He must be the stillness.

He knows that what
he needs, will come.

He must be ready for it.

This morning's rain runs
off the slate of his back.

He understands, somehow.

The rain is the river, and
The river is the fish, and

The fish is himself.

The Last Time We All Saw Nannie in Gerritsen Beach

Nannie Lovejoy's house
sat at the foot of a pier.
Her front yard was a bulkhead.

In the near distance,
the ribbon of madness
called The Belt Parkway
girdled the great belly of Brooklyn.

Nannie was there with Aunt Dot,
grown permanently crabby from
living a long life with her mother.

Nannie sat fixed in her chair,
hair deep white, and far too old
to bother standing to greet.
Who knew her name was Sadie,
short for Sarah, her own mother's name?

Richard lived alone downstairs,
in the basement apartment.
He had once belonged to someone,
but now he was not right.
We only knew him as Cousin Richard,
who lived his life downstairs,
hanging onto his circumstances
by only a thread.

Aunt Dot made us tea and
offered simple cookies from a box,
happy to see her little sister, or not.

We didn't stay long,
even with the thought
that they would all be dead
before another day like this.

We lived by my Grandfather's clock.
He never forgetting that
to Dot and to Nannie, he would
always be that Miserable Guinea Bastard
who had married my Grandmother.

They say The Lovejoys were once
colonial aristocrats in Maine,
with land and with treasure
enough for a kingdom.

Now it was just Nannie,
in her chair by a bulkhead
in Gerritsen Beach, preparing
her next complaint for Aunt Dot.

Before her, jammed into
her tiny front room, overlooking
a hundred yards of oily water,
three generations of people
she had spawned, and

That Miserable Guinea Bastard,
hand in his pocket, and
jingling his car keys.

Watching People Cook on TV

Makes me hungry every time.
I suppose that is the intent,
the chef torturing by temptation.

They make it all facile as
the knife, sharp and precisely placed.
All manner of delightful stuff
stirring with spoons of wood.

It is all even worse to endure,
directed by the slow intonations
of a Frenchman or Italian.

The stock reducing between commercials.
Everything alloying and rising unerringly.
The sauce, the seduction, the dénouement,
The coursing of velvets, causing
the tastebuds to perspire then weep aloud.

And it all transpires in
twenty-seven minutes or less.
The previously prepared dish
emerging as a Queen from her carriage.
All delivered to a platter like
the virgin on her wedding night.

While we, the sad and starved,
left to our common yearnings,
resolve our desires with a cola and
what's left of the bag of chips.

The Sandpiper at the River

after Samuel Menashe

The Sandpiper stabs at
inconspicuous stuff,
Not convincing himself
that he's had quite enough.

With decided cadence
he's bobbing his bottom,
Tallying time taken
peck-pecking at flotsam.

Adjudging the rocks have
naught left to be eaten,
The Sandpiper gently
dips both of his feet in.

These Walking Sticks

for David Ferry

I have these two canes.
I keep them beside the umbrella,
In the umbrella stand at
the top of the stairs.

I have it from my Grandmother,
a woman of eloquent memory,
They belonged to
her Father's sister, Gertrude.
and her husband, Will Keenan.

They are not much more
than wisps of hickory,
Polished by the touch
of those who've held them.
Simple and elegant as any branch.

The heads of them, slight enough
to nest in the palm of a child,
Make me suspect I am
from people of modest stature.

I was told Gertrude and Will had
a twenty year betrothal.
Waiting, as the proper did, for
the weddings of elder sisters.

Grace wed young, Sister May
cloistered with The Sisters of Mercy.
Josephine was left a spinster.

But Gertrude and Will did have their day,
Though at an age beyond fruitfulness,
when most might be spoiling grandchildren.

These many years later,
there is a grand
wedding portrait in my head,
I will never get to see.

My Great Grandfather John
and his other three sisters,
Adorned in high collars and a
reticent Victorian contentment.

All of them set into stillness,
beside Mr. and Mrs. Will Keenan.
Wedded in their early dotage.
Living out this one part,
of all that might have been.

Posed gently beside one another.
Joined with a muted tenderness,
and leaning on these very sticks.

The Last Supper of Judas Iscariot

Judas was right
to wait until after dessert.
If only for the Savior of Mankind
to finish his coffee and pie.

He knew his Master
would not be happy
about any of it.

While his dimwit brothers,
shared a glass of Port,
He, whose name would
be called betrayer, said
He would pass, thanks.

Judas was right, but
He hated long goodbyes.
I'll see you in the garden, later.
There's a guy in town
who owes me money.

The Lord and Savior spoke:
I've got a long day tomorrow.
How about one more joke,
And we'll call it a night.

Then he leaned onto
his elbows and he asked,
Did you all hear the one
about the guy, who thinks
he's seen a ghost?

To Harpo

You really
had us all
bewildered, as you
carried on in your
too-big trench coat,
the pockets of your
trousers full of
who knows what.

The men we knew
did not have
hair like that,
an obscene
cacophony of curls
under an abused
top hat, which
folded over
like an accordion.

Who but you
could produce
a live chicken, or
a full length of salami, or
a lighted blowtorch
from his vest pocket?
Your perfect silence
made us strain,
hoping to hear even
the tiniest of murmurs.

But the only sound was
the sounds of birds, which
emerged from a magical
arrangement of knuckles.
Oh, How just your move-
ments
could fill a room with chaos.

But when you wrapped
yourself around the curlicue
of that harp, and
then when you played,
you played
with the angels.

When Nothing Happens

Shelter Island, New York, 2007

I have stared out
through this window before.
Many times.
Who knows
the sums of such things?

I was there this morning,
a fresh mug of coffee
sending the aroma of waking
up from the table beside me.

Yesterday, the trees
were the waving arms
of children at a parade.
The sunrise was
a golden flood.

In Winter, the finches
were the ghosts of Spring.
The frozen pond
a tomb for the sky.

The Christmas cactus was
the ebon night above us
on The Fourth of July, and
the hill which lifts this house
fell away from the porch
like the falter toward eternity.

But on this day,
the glass is only glass.
The rain is only the rain.
This morning is but the
last of last night.
The cats are just cats.
The leaves of the laurel
look as they do, and

I am only a man
in an old robe,
cradling a cooled cup,
capped pen in his pocket,
and likely to be late
for work.

Some Kind of Sonnet for a Mayfly

for Michael Arcieri

If it be true what learned people say,
The Mayfly lives for but a day.
I'll not shed even the tiniest tear,
Or wish he'd make it one more year.
Instead I would concentrate on just how grand,
To live without next week's demand.

And among the simple Mayfly facts is,
He never once has to file his taxes.
Or contemplate the waning moon,
Or anticipate any time but soon.
Never repay but only borrow,
Or check the weather for tomorrow.

It might be luxury, if I may be bold,
To be unconcerned about growing old.
No time for beddy-by, nor alarms to be set,
No time for longing or for regret.
Not to mention that on his day in May,
He might decide to alight or just fly away.

Another thing any Mayfly knows,
He won't need to shop for winter clothes.
Never wondering while watching the setting sun,
Why living seems over before it's begun.
The Mayfly is the only who can truly say,
That the Mayfly has so truly had his day.

At eight in the morn his youth would flower,
Old age a twenty-fifth or twenty-sixth hour.
Never needing to strain his brain to remember,
Where he was on the twenty-fourth of September.
Oh Mayfly how strangely fortunate,
Is the lifetime brief and immediate.

Mayfly whose life is so fleetly fleeting,
Might seem so surely worth repeating.

Patti Smith Does The Hamptons

Patti Smith, you
are not looking good.
You must know that.
The years have
weathered you like
a Cape Cod shingle.

I suppose you
are as angry at this life
as you ever were, back
when you crawled in
from The Jersey Suburbs
to hang in The Bunker
with Burroughs and
Ginsberg and Warhol
and Mapplethorpe.

The Original
Bowery Fag-Hag.

I can only imagine
the suffering endured,
dragging a brush
through that hair.
But you stayed on
your feet last night,
despite the teetering,
sustaining yourself
with a bottle of
Poland Spring Water.

If I had had
the chance to
actually speak to you,
I would have told you that
I think myself a poet too.

And if there had been
any hope of a reply,
I might have asked
you why you
found it necessary to
spit on my new shoe.

Dancers

Even as we live, it is
the dead we romance.
Leading them onto
the ballroom floor.

Placing a soft hand on
the swale of their backs.
We guide them in
slow and careful circles.
Over the lacquered wood.
Our cheeks pressed to theirs.

There is something
about that cold.
And the eyes.
Like unlit rooms.

We mourn them.
We sing them all the
sad and luscious songs.

They mourn us as well.
Watching from a balcony,
in the ballroom of our believing.

It is something
they will confess to us
someday.
Just after
asking us to dance.

It's Like OMG!

my children
use their thumbs
to converse with
invisible people

they speak
a language
with no words
a shorthand
of the hands

sometimes
I try using
my voice to
interrupt them

yet they contin-
ue wandering
in a place
with no sound

where thoughts
become reflexes
and god exists
as a single letter

i love you

to Karen

Since I dared say
those words for
the first time, to you,
they have hollowed,
useless as a goblet
after the wine is drunk.

My throat, my lips
no longer
form them well.
I have offered them
too many times
to the unworthy,
who begged them
of me and were gone.

I am a man
attempting feebly
to work words into
the figures of birds.
They have no flight
beyond my wishes.

For you, the only one
who has mattered,
I've not the words,
nor the tools to
fashion them any longer.
Because of you,
the world will
never be the same.

I cannot say why,
still I know.

Instead, take my fingers
over your shoulder, as
we fall to our sleeping.
Take the darkness, how it
keeps us there, within it.
Take how this morning's
light falls over our roof
and splashes over the trees.
Take all the colors.

We share time
and nourishment. We
mingle our breaths
and our dreaming. We
look to no past.

I love you is not enough.
Some things defy the naming.

Let me rest my head
on your shoulder and
rest yours on mine.
Take my glance, it
contains much more.
I have no words
more true, more tender
than what is found
in that vast silence.

Fireflies

to a girl from Pipestone, Minnesota

There was the white house
with the tiny rooms,

Beside the blonde wheat
which danced with a wind,
which came late each day
to carry in the gloaming.

On those warmed nights
July spilt with stars,

There were the fireflies
that played against the
flecked blackness and the
whispered hissing of voices.

And there was the road
which led to places which
could not be seen.

Above my head as I ran,
over the leaning wheat,
a horizon too far to be considered.

Now in the distance of years.
cradling a glass of wine to warm me,

There is the river that runs the night,
and the fireflies on new shoots of

Primrose, Lupine and Butterfly Weed,
beneath these abiding White Pines.

My head against a chair that rocks me,
I am thinking of wheat and roads.
A house filled with ghosts and strangers,
the dark alighting around me.

My hand cradles a glass filled with light,
that time has clarified and sweetened.

Elegy for Killer Kowalski

Dead 18 August, 2008, at 81

I was just a boy
when I first saw you
inside our old Philco.

A mass of a man in tights,
and a skullcap which
put a bolt of lightning
on the center of your forehead.
You had a chin like a Buick.

I loved to watch you
storm yourself around
the roped ring,
stalking that other man,
then plowing him
face first to the floor.

Oh yes, I grimaced knowing
what was coming.
The dreaded *Claw Hold*.
Mashing your great fingers
into his doughy gut, twisting
until the contest was finished.

There was that day at
The Montreal Forum in '54,
where you faced down Yukon Eric
and earned your name.

Walter, you never killed anyone.
But no one had ever seen
a man's ear ripped from his head,
and sent flying through the air,
quite like that.

Human History

in memory of Howard Zinn

It's a sad life
in a sad world

Where few
know the truth

And no one
will say it.

Squandering the precious
Defying death

We destroy
all we touch

Singing our songs
as we go.

Fiona

Of the two, it's the red cat
who accompanies me everywhere.
Sleeping at my head, across
my chest, between my knees
in the long darkness,
Comforted by things of me
I cannot sense.

She watches as I
assemble myself for the day,
and again as I
undress before the dark.
She surely wonders where I am
in the in-between.

She even attempts speech,
a language of monosyllables.
But only when
she has something to say.
She knows I will attend
her story, told in a language
I neither speak nor read,
yet understand.

It is elegant in simplicity.
She is a cat who
wishes to be a person.
And I am a person who
wishes she were.

A Small Request

I told the
girl in the green smock

That I
wanted a small cup of coffee.

She might
not have understood me.

Instead, she pointed
my attention to a high place

On the wall
behind her, which suggested

A complex choice
was before me, one which

Might best be made
after a cup of coffee.

I turned
back to face her again

The girl
in the green smock.

She asked
what I would like, but

I did not
see it on her wall.

She asked
what I might want that

I did not
see written up on her wall.

I said
a small cup of coffee.

But she
just made the same response.

So, I told her
I would have a Pepsi instead.

She said Coke,
She only had Coke.

Then she asked,
What size?

A Gold Case

I have a gold watch.
Bought in *Île de la Cité*
on my last *Lune de Miel.*

It runs well, but
twenty-three minutes
fast every day.

I look at it, but
I never know what
time it might really be.

It is always
sometime
just prior.

Like me, my wife
loves the watch,
just as she loved *Paris.*

She often tells me
that she loves
me as well, except

For my always
being early, thinking
I am right on time.

A Question for their Gods

for Phil Appleman

You made them lithe.
vertical with sinew.
cunning and swift.
Given to tenderness.

They fell in love
with the night sky,
then filled it with gods
of very many names.

They made lives from
rocks and raindrops.
Walked their way through
dust and through mud.

They carried their things
across savannah and sea.
Ascended, wondering, to the
far sides of the mountains.

Under the midday sun.
From shade to shade.
Their purpose, the horizon.
Their backs to the night.

But why create so many,
with so little to sustain them?
And like you, capable of
such ruin and cruelties?

Ascendency

for Samuel Menashe at The Bower in Central Park

His eye is
upon
the sparrow.

But

The sparrow
has
no clue.

The sparrow,
unlike
The Almighty,

has

more important
things
to do.

Rewiring Paradise

for David Lambert

We, who are
new to this place,
Must be fit for
the great untangling of things.

Switches which do not switch.
Pipes which no longer convey.
Vines of wire hanging unattached.
And the many contraptions
whose purpose will die a mystery.

It is what has been left to us.
We who must conform
the stuff of past lives
to this peculiar place.

This morning
I went out to determine
why the pole light,
Which stands sentinel
at the foot of our drive,
No longer casts
its beacon over the street.

Another lead to be followed.

There, laid along the trunk
of this white oak,
it has disappeared.

Engulfed over
half a lifetime by the
healing nature of bark.

In the newfangled world,
with all things yet indiscernible,
It was the god of Abraham,
who prompted the light from the dark.

In the woods before our house
It is a white oak, unacquainted with
the names of gods,
who tacitly adjures me
on behalf of the dark.

One more struggle and The Lady will be free.

LE FIGARO, Paris, 1884

Portrait of Madame X

by John Singer Sargent

Surely, there are those
who might be given
to pondering the days
of privileged ladies.
Long mornings
and afternoons in wait,
while her gentleman
is off tipping a flute
or slurping an oyster.

Today I powdered my décolleté.
I drew my coiffure back tight and
affixed this diamond clip.
To my lips a carefully placed
touch of a rich vermillion.
If you care to know,
it was just the same yesterday,
and the day before that one.
Losing my good sleep each night
anxious, over the first question
you always pose, Sir:

"Madame Gautreau,
Do you recall
how you were standing
when we stopped?"

One can only gaze
out and through this window
for just so long.
It's only the day's light that changes.
I have clutched at my fan and
the drape of this gown, for lifetimes.
Seeking my relief and my balance
upon the pedestal of one thumb.

But My Dear Sir,
There is such aching
in the balls of my pitiable feet.
My neck might never again
be set straight between
my head and shoulders. Then,
there is that looming space
above the mantle where
my youth will be forever hung.
Have you dared consider
the possible calamity
of my husband's disapproval?
And if he should balk at your fee?

If you please, Good Sir,
my strap is about to slip.
Might we pause
for just a small moment?
I swear, I will have the head
of that damnable couturier.

To Debbie After I Had
Already Eaten The Octopusses

Last night, over a pizza,
I told you how, last week
I had eaten a marinated
baby octopus or two
in the Japanese restaurant.
Actually I ate four of them,
all tiny and tender and still,
(except for the one
which was a bit tough).

I told you that I
had first hesitated, seeing
them there huddled together
on the square china plate.
But I didn't want to
embarrass myself
in front of my wife,
(who was unsure about
the idea from the start),
or the little Japanese girl
who had served them up.

I felt like a crow, or worse,
some kind of viper,
robbing them of their
forever unfulfilled lives.
I left one there, just
to show that I wasn't
heartless, even in my hunger,
capable of the truest mercies.

But then you told me
of the program that you
had just watched, on
The Remarkable Octopus,
how they were so smart,
possessed of *true sentiments,*
tender creatures, and
almost human you said.

I suppose we could have
also wept for the pizza.

Instead I thought that, perhaps
those babies might have
one day survived to become the
TERRIBLE GIANTS OF THE DEEP.
Lunging up to grasp a ship of refugees,
or even eco-tourists on holiday.
Dragging them down screaming
into a grave of briny blackness.

So, now I prefer to be:
That brave man who had
saved four fine ships, and
the lives of many scores of
old women and babies,
on the high savage seas
fleeing places of hunger and tyrants.
A great man with this one regret:

One should not trifle with monsters.

I should have eaten the last
of those *wicked little bastards,*
and asked for a second helping.

Now, A Month Beyond

We would like it to be different.
But it can never be different.

We try to talk about it even more,
As if the words were a salve, but
there are not the right words, not
even the wrong words arranged well.

We want to go back, to do it
all again, but with our eyes wide.
We would have listened for noises.
We might have detected
the scent of it in the room.

We would like it to begin again
from where it left us off.
But we will not find you there.
We will not locate ourselves there.
We have come to know too much.

The very air has been fouled, the light eclipsed.
Squinting will not clarify any of it, nor bending to it.
We know well we have come too late.
The clock has circled past midnight.

We might have stopped you,
but the door was locked
from the inside, as you had left it.
We might have found you in time but
you were done with time and
the key was in your pocket.

We can only hope to sort fragments,
for that small hope to remedy this despair.
We would like it to be different, but today,
like yesterday, and like the day before that day,
this thing derived is just the same.

If there were reason, we might not have to bear it.
We can only hope to learn to bear it, to bear all of it.
But you took your reasons with you, and
You left us here, wishing for it to be different.
What chance do we have?
Of all things, why did you choose that?

Together and Waiting

The people in the waiting room at the hospital
cannot help but wonder just what is wrong
with everyone else.

The old woman in the borrowed wheelchair.
The man with the bandaged right hand.
The brown child whose mother is crying.

Someone has taped paper flowers to the wall.

A person in a green outfit will come for them soon.
They will learn, one at a time, the names of

The old woman in the borrowed wheelchair.
The man with the bandaged right hand.
The brown child whose mother is crying.

They all just want to be O.K.,
for the person in the green outfit to tell them so.
Then they can be happy again, happy
to be gone from the waiting room at the hospital.

And they can forget
the colors of the paper flowers taped to the wall,
and the names they had learned one at a time.

Missing People

On my television,
they're looking for
another missing person.
Way out in the desert
and in the woods.

With dogs and
sharp sticks and
special cameras
which take pictures
at night.

Whole towns are looking.

In ponds and
along roadways.
In drainage ditches
and down in old wells.
They say that
they won't stop
until they find them,
even if they have
become just a pile
of chalky bones.

You can see
the photos of them
on power poles
all across America.

They look familiar,
as if we just
saw them behind us
at the supermarket
or sitting, reading
at the bus stop.

There is one in
my yard right now,
crouching behind
one of the shrubs.

When I asked,
they said they
prefer to be missing.
And who am I
to argue with them?
I was missing once.

There is something
to be said for it.

Minus Twelve

It's daybreak, and today,
the brass thermometer,
Resolute beside the
kitchen's window, reads:

Minus Twelve Fahrenheit.

Below the window,
The Warner River proffers
an anomalous steam,

The mists of which have
encased the lissome boughs
of the cherry trees in glass.

It is a struggle
which astonishes.

The struggle between
Continuance and Capitulation.

Between
the water,
and the ice.

Between a bottomless sky
and the
hushed tombs of the winter.

Minding The Pits

for Catherine Arcure

An olive and an apricot,
contain a day that
was dry and hot.

And drops of mist
by clouds relieved,
Like the brackish tears
the widow grieved.

For them did
poets dare invent,
A word so rare
as succulent.

Yet in their heart
there lives alone,
This silent and
solitary stone.

As dense as
any secret be,
Until one reflects
upon the tree.

Life Now

It is not so different, really.
There are oaks and wildflowers,
and stones in our garden.
In the house where we sleep,
there is a case of books,
and they are our books.

The sunlight is most
beautiful in the early morning
just before the world gets busy.
There is work to be done
during each of our days, as well.
Work which makes us feel
tired and contented.

There is also water.
Not empty and still,
but thin and silken over
and amidst the big rocks.
All the long day and night
It makes a sound like wind.
It travels while our travels
have ended, Here.

There is a stately heron, who
comes to fish in the noon.
Yesterday I saw the hummingbird,
only minutes after I had reached
to hang his red feeder.

I was pleased at his arrival.
I spent a small time wondering,
how he knew where to find us,
just as he had done in
all those green summers,
far away.

Letter to Siv

for Siv Cedering – 24 November, 2007

This afternoon, at
The Funeral Home
in East Hampton,
they all talked
about you.

You were gone,
and
No one knew where.

Outside,
on The Highway,
it was the day
after Thanksgiving,

Limpid and crisp
with a provoking wind.

The cars streamed by
as in the
beach days of August.

At Twin Oaks,
the horses
bowed down to
the alfalfa, the broad gate
was latched.

Beyond
the grayed fence,
was that
silence you cherished.

The one with many voices.

It floated among
the sculpture, settling over
the green and stone.

It was the cape
you made for
the shoulders of your life.

But now,
we draw back tears
against
the din of slow traffic.

There are things
we have been
asked to believe,
that we cannot.

It is all too much.

Today, we chose
to not think about
where
you might have gone.

We think instead,
on places where we
might still find you.

In Mashomack

I want you to know that
all things are present
to those who know patience.
Among these tangled paths
all things have become clear.

Along their course,
I have felt the Earth
rise and fall beneath my tread,
tasted a wind that carried
salt and seed and snow,
made love to the air with
the dragonflies, finches and hawks.
I have witnessed a sharp sun in January,
and a sky obscured by clouding,
just beyond the noon in July.

Shorelines, saplings and fawns.
Dust and mud and wildflowers.

I will retrace these paths
even when my legs betray me,
even when I become unsure.
For I have come to trust the birds
and the limbs of the trees,
and the grasses which lean over the path.

Even as the quiet nights are folding me
safely into my very deepest dreams,
I will know these ways and I will be
walking, ever walking.
When you come here,
look for me.

A Fortnight on the Queen Victoria

15th - 25th October, 2011

Our days
have become one,
upon this blue sea,
aboard this
blue ship.

Punctuated
by a sun,
which climbs
from the sea,
and then
succumbs again.

All our ports
contained by
steep rock,
and cascades
of tiny houses.

Their names
have become
an alphabet,
decidedly
indecipherable.

But what is it we
so surely know?
There is much
to this world.

That we too,
are among
the strange,
and the unfamiliar.

Adrift.

On the Dying of Amy Winehouse

Among us, there are
those who will not make it.

Those who will
contend with mortality,
Wrapping themselves
around it,
Unable to let go.

We watch them
as prey through a sight.
Cheer them
as the mob below,
Looks up at
the man on the ledge.

We are unsure
what to hope for.

We stand by
as they put
the pain into
their limbs and lungs.

We take what we desire.
They understand how
want has no confines.

But too soon
the bed is emptied of lovers.
And we are left
with the despair that knows,

What we do to one another,
is still less, than that
which we do to ourselves.

The Dusts of Pompeii

17 October, 2011, at the Bay of Napoli on The Queen Victoria

The dusts of Pompeii
are upon my feet.
Captured time
in fine ash.

Jupiter's stone columns
against the cerulean sky,
Ever upright, as they
were that last day.

Rooms where children
slept, among distant dreams.
Hearths where the baker
turned straw to
flour, flour to gold.
Sailors straddled the shore,
drank full, and reclined into
the arms of harlots.

Once, April rains fell
through the rutted stone,
faltering to the primeval sea.
Once, Apollo poured sunlight
over the hillsides.

Here is this day, just
as in some once-long-ago,
beside the tranquil Vesuvius,
Maker of quakes
and tombs.

One Cool Cat

On the final day of
The Davisville Flea Market,
the crowd and the fare were sparse.
The morning sun was having
little effect on the gathered frost.

On a table of multifarious treasures,
perhaps only hours from a trash bin,
was the tiny black-porcelain kitten,
playing a tiny porcelain saxophone.

I wondered at just what
he might play, if he could.
Whether he preferred
Coltrane over Charlie Parker.

Why as a young kittycat,
aspirant to the musical life,
He passed over the accordion and ukulele?
And why not the cello or French horn?

This morning there was
no point in troubling him.

He looked content, even inspired,
tiny lips on his sax,
seeming prepared to wail,
forever contained by contrivance,
and glistening with frost.

Arrhythmias

for the good people at Concord Hospital – 5 August 2012

It would be easy
to hate this place,
How very tiny we feel
within the enormity of it.

But it has taken us
into its rooms,
Set us apart
where we can watch,

The nurses and technicians
of all names, festooned
in their pinks and yellows,
their cheerful cartoon prints.

They have determined to
care for the afflicted and
the stricken among us.

They make the measures
and the counts, stay awake
the long nights, while we
attempt rest between
the lifeless walls, nod off
to the songs of crickets
in their machines.

We take pause on the
landings of our long descent,
And bargain with the
dealer of our decrepitude.

It would be easy
to hate this place.
The fluorescent evenings
and disheveled sleep.

The bins of things
wrapped in plastic.
Our clothes folded
into an uneasy slumber,
inside a borrowed drawer.

You see, we do not
want to come here,
but we must. Driven
by that familiar fear,
the one which makes us
who we have always been.

We do not wish to
grow frail and feeble,
in need of the others
who will mark our path.

So we resent it all.
The tubing and linens.
The taking of deep breaths.
The lying still, attempting to heal.

It would be easy
to hate this place,
Thinking of the bed
at home half empty, as

We take careful note of what
minutes appear like
in passing.

February Nineteenth, New Hampshire in the Year without Snow

for Dennis and Lynda Crawford

Here, within the breast of February,
the sun is alighting and large, blinding
as it slips to a place the hill conceals.

But the ground is dressed
in cloaks of browned leaves,
relinquished in the long past fall.
The Warner River is easing,
free of late winter ice.

This will be the year
we will recall, when we awaited
the snows that did not come.
The sky, a bottomless blue.

When the cold was
not our cold at all,
the earth dispossessed of sleep.

This will be the year
we believed we could hear
the daffodils, wondering among themselves,
Is it time? Is it time, now?

Sons and Fathers

In their odd hats and coats,
they practice to be their own fathers.

In their hard-soled shoes,
they desire to be a definition.

They understand what might have been,
that never was,
their voices resonant with echoes.

Driven by an unnamed madness,
to do what must be done.

In the pale breath of a swelling moonlight,
their children cradled by the darkness,

They seem to be near, but
they might be anywhere else.

If you live long enough,
you too, will come to claim it.

The table set without chairs.
The awareness shared in our descent.

And in our falling life, everything
will seem taller than it was, yet

Never so tall as it needed to be.

A Poem of Necessity

Today I am grieving, but
not for any certain reason.
It is Saturday at a country house.
No one should be grieving here.

But it happens that way, at times.
It is a thing we do to ourselves.

Afterall, people sing in prisons.
They laugh in rooms with the dying.
Surely things end, but they
begin as well, don't they?

Perhaps I am not grieving
for today, but for yesterday.
I recall clearly when it was
right there before me, now
I am unsure where I put it.

It is not unlike the wind, which
comes and goes, or the leaves
it takes from these trees, which
accumulate in layers of loss.
It's not for what I can recall,
but only for what I cannot.

It is there in my mirror, in the
face I have come to own.
The face which has become
a gray shroud for my youth.

So much for us to know,
all the more to be imagined.
Surely we should not
spare time to grieve.
Our time passes, and we
must pass with it.

What strange things, these musings
which can cause the eyes to fill.
Facing how much of it is bygone.

Last night, in this house, our cats
walked the floor above our bed,
through the length of the dark,
while no one was watching,

They traveled the night.

The Man from an Unknown Place

Along the waterfront
in Old Bombay,
Beside the
Gateway of India,

Stood a man, dressed
in a black kurta pajama,
who asked where
I was from.

I said Boston.
He said he
had never heard
of it.

I said, How
about New York?
He just said,
"No."

In the Streets of Mumbai

for Ankur and Khushbu Oswal — January, 2013

The dusts of India have
lain down upon everything,
Concealing the writing
on the walls, Weighing
down the sagging rooftops,
Choking the sun and the machines,
Veiling the fifty million
brown feet of Mumbai.

The dogs shake a dusty shake.
The cows low a dusty low.
Teak, sable-haired men
chase it with wispy brooms.

It is only the women
who seem immune to it all,
Draped in pastel silks,
their flowing hems
keeping it from them.

This morning, in the
streets of Mumbai,
spattered over the chaos,
they are the shed petals of
jasmine, rose and marigold,
fallen from the garlands
of a bride and her groom.

Newtown

15 December, 2012

The sounds we hear,
are the noises we make.

Of doors slamming shut,
Of lights put out,
Of the flesh being torn from us.

Tranquility has no place left to it.
We have lost the notes
of the song that starts the day.

We replace it all
with the expressions of the lost.
More sirens and church bells.

The beckoning to our angels.
The laments to the indifferent clouds.

Can we bear to
see ourselves yet again, in
all that's been vanished?

Who among us has words
to explain the slaughter
of the babies of strangers?

Who are these people
we claim to not know,
But us?

The Galapagos Islands

November, 2012

Here in Black Turtle Cove,
the morning's waters are
low and smooth,

Broken only by the
soft stroking of Julio's white paddle
at the panga's ropey prow.

It draws us forward, into
the angling sunrise,
closer to the mangrove,
dense green against the sharp light,

Suspended by a woven nest
of gnarled woods,
lying like a garland against
the water's edge.

Here on the island called Santa Cruz,
the ancient consecrated turtles cross,
from the South Pacific into the
blue-emerald shallows.

They are willed here by that force,
which adjures them to
the godless Eternal, and
calls them to the dance of life.

Psychotherapy

No one ever,
gets the parents
they deserve.

Born as we are,
with empty bellies,
and filled with
insatiable hankering.

Our childhoods,
become a bowl
of broth
with no meat.

All of it
seasoned with a
touch too much
pepper and brine.

Then, desperate,
we squander our
lives in search
of butter,

For all the
bread we never
had.

From Farnan's Well

for Yvonne Henry

I've been down to Ballymeeny
to speak with the wind
      and the dead.
Beside a
   smooth swale of shore
which slid like a penstroke
   away from Ben Bulben.
I stood
      at the top of a lane
       rutted by rain
and the farmer's wood wheels.
Humbled
by a horizon
    which birthed the days.
Against
   a sky of rare cyan,
the clouds tumbled like
     cream into tea.
So I looked
     to the glen where
your freshet fell from
      the hills.
I looked
   for you, Delia Kilcullen,
filling your bucket at
     St. Farnan's Well,
your feet,   like mine,
   wet with this mud.

I looked for
             your brothers and your
Father calling for
the strayed lamb, and your
Mother feeding
             turf to the fire.

They were all
             so young and you
but a girl when you left them,
             wild and unsettled
as the briar among these
             well-placed stones.
A girl who knew not far
             beyond this darkened door
lived all the stars which
ever were.
You listened dearly to the
             whispers of waters
never stilled,   and with
your bucket at each aurora, you
imagined the sun might lift the sea,
             as once more,
the dark overcame
             the Sligo hills.

Once Home

for Annie Henry nee Kilcullen

Settled against
a trough in a hillside,
the narrow arched
doorway led southward,
backed against the sea
and shell-strewn shore.
Would it have been
your father or his who
collected and carried
each jagged stone?
Who laid them edge to
edge, corner to crenel,
until they were composed
just tall enough to contain
the height of a man?

Once a roof of crisp thatch
angled to banish
the wind and pelts of rain,
it has finally succumbed
to the vagaries of day and
the sky. Walls once sure,
downed and crumbled,
become but a simple byre
for another man's cows.
Now they and we
stand overtaken by bog iris,
new daisies and fodder.
The great struggles and small,
the turning seasons, the fiddling
and stepping long ended.

And, what is gone after all?
Not your name.
Not the leaning Ben Bulben.
Neither the river nor sky.
Not the serenity beside this rill.
And surely not the sea,
the ancient incessant sea.

After Keats' Ode to a Nightingale

Prepare for me the feast divine,
a table so resplendent.
A place to sip the timeless wine,
from the vineyards of contentment.

I dread not nightfall's mystery,
from this vantage in the twilight.
As did I then a youthful me,
bathed in morning's dew light.

Mine ear is cocked in deference,
to the far winds beckoning.
To let my eternity commence,
from this faithless mortal reckoning.

Oh, Nightingale at my garden's gate,
serenading sweet the fractured hours.
Your strains do cause my soul elate,
making the rumbling darkness cower.

Dim Forever, be this my final thought?
Mine ears filled with this perfection?
Is this raspy growl what time has wrought?
Myself the furrowed face in this reflection?

Oh Age, cruel as the driver's whip,
the stinging winter lies cross my back.
The fire of life falling from my grasp,
my pastel sunrise must fade to black.

Shadow, spare me not your insistence,
nor death, the brine in this falling tear.
My heart will cease without resistance,
sure my own day of darkness nears.

With this toiling my gnarly fingers ache,
expression eludes me like a virgin.
Now my face burns with each icy flake,
of these snows silent and urgent.

Oh, mock me no more you wistful youth,
cast no fretful eye upon me,
Take heed all, truths senescence speaks,
words spoken too soon for thee.

To The Bug Who Perished in My Drink

for Shane MacGowan

To the bug who just per---
ished in my drink:
You have caused me
to take......
a pause....
for a think.........

I might have ad---
vised that before
you begin it,
Better you should
die of the drink
rather than
in it.

Though liquor
can be our mortal di---
version, it's surely
quicker n simpler
to die by im---
mersion.

While I con---
sider *You* now my
sad little ghost,
Howzabout
one more round
for a toast?

To all those *cre---*
atures both
humble and great.
and
To the plea---
sures of sha---
ring a drink
with a mate.

DANIEL THOMAS MORAN, born in New York City in 1957, is the author of six volumes of poetry, the most recent of which, *Looking for the Uncertain Past*, was published by Poetry Salzburg at The University of Salzburg in 2006. He holds a Bachelor's Degree in Biology from Stony Brook University (1979) and a Doctorate in Dental Surgery from Howard University (1983). He has read widely throughout New York City and Long Island and has done readings in Ireland, Italy, Austria, Great Britain, at The Library of Congress, and at The United Nations. He was Poet Laureate of Suffolk County, New York, from 2005 to 2007.

His work has appeared in such prestigious journals as *Confrontation, The Recorder, Nassau Review, Oxford, Hawaii Pacific Review, Commonweal, Parnassus, Opium, Istanbul Literature Review, Pedestal, Rattapallax, LUNGFULL, Poetry Salzburg Review, The New York Times, The Journal of The American Medical Association*, and *The Norton Critical Anthology on Darwin*. From 1997-2005 he served as Vice-President of The Walt Whitman Birthplace Association in West Hills, New York where he instituted The Long Island School of Poetry Reading Series and has been Literary Correspondent to Long Island Public Radio where he hosted *The Long Island Radio Magazine*.

His work has been nominated for a Pushcart Prize on ten occasions. He was profiled on New York Public Television's *Setting the Stage*, and on *The Poet and The Poem* from The Library of Congress hosted by Grace Cavalieri. He was profiled in the 2009 edition of *Poet's Market*. He is a participating writer to *The Password Project*, an international collaboration between visual artists and writers based in Austria.

In 2005 he was appointed Poet Laureate by The Legislature of Suffolk County, New York, the birthplace of Walt Whitman.

His work has been translated into German, Spanish, Romanian, Chinese and Italian. He has been listed in Who's Who in America since 2000. He is a member of PEN American and has been ordained a Celebrant by The American Humanist Association. He edited The Light of City and Sea, An Anthology of Suffolk County Poetry 2006 (Street Press). His collected papers are being archived by The Frank Melville Library at Stony Brook University in New York. In 2006 he was inducted into The Massapequa High Schools Hall of Fame. He is a founding member of Irish American Writers and Artists, Inc. and a member of The Association of Literary Critics, Scholars and Writers. He is the father of Lindsay, Ashley and Gregory. From 2009 to 2013 he was Clinical Assistant Professor of General Dentistry at Boston University's School of Dental Medicine where he delivered the 2011 Commencement Address, and twice received The Outstanding Clinical Faculty Award from his students. He and his wife Karen live on the Warner River in Webster, New Hampshire.